BUTTERFLIES,
ANGELS AND ROSES

BUTTERFLIES, ANGELS AND ROSES

messages of hope and healing
from a bereaved mother's heart

by
Frances Wohlenhaus-Munday

The Marlys Ann Wohlenhaus Foundation, Inc.
Isanti, Minnesota

COVER ART: Neverne Covington, Saint Petersburg, Florida

Library of Congress Cataloging in Publication Data:

Wohlenhaus-Munday, Frances
    Butterflies, Angels and Roses
    1. Healing grief   2. Death of a child
    3. Bereavement Counseling
ISBN 1-879535-21-1 Paper

Published by
The Marlys Ann Wohlenhaus Foundation, Inc.
http://www.murdercanbesolved.com
P. O. Box 423
Isanti, Minnesota
in cooperation with
Skipjack Press, Inc.
Ocean Pines, Maryland

Printed in the United States of America

Foreword

Years ago Fran and I heard a man talk about Psalm 23, quoting the part that says, "Though I walk through the valley of the shadow of death, I will fear no evil." What we remember is not the substance of his talk, but one phrase. He said, "When you see someone who has walked through that valley, see if the mourner has picked a flower on the way." Since then we've tried to find the flowers in life and share our bouquet with others.

Butterflies, angels, and roses have accompanied us in the years I have walked with Marlys' mom through the valleys and over the hills of our life together. Fran honors Marlys by following what Marlys wrote to her mom in the last greeting card she gave her in Marlys' far too short life. "Mom. Be happy!"

This book is a testament to a grieving mother who chose to pick the flowers on her journey, and share them with us. In Fran's own words, "If I can't have Marlys back, and I know I can't in this world, I want to be healed."

Fran's symbols of butterflies, angels, and roses offer comfort to those who mourn. Join her as she shares these messages of hope and healing.

Jack Munday
May, 2003
Casa Mariposa
Isanti County, Minnesota

Acknowledgments

I would like to thank the following people and organizations who have been important in my healing and the writing of this book:

My husband, John Steffen Munday, who has been beside me during my most difficult moments in my journey since 1979. He has been supportive in all that I have done to keep Marlys' memory alive and to seek justice for her. His strength gave me the courage to reach out when I didn't think I had any strength left.

My son, Raymond W. Wohlenhaus, my first born whose life was shattered by his sister's death. Ray has shown me that siblings hurt too, and now he and I can walk together in the love that Marlys left behind for us to share.

My daughter, Lynn Wohlenhaus Winger, my youngest, who misses her sister and best friend. Lynn became a Registered Nurse in honor of Marlys and is also helping those in grief because she understands their pain. What a gift to give others in memory of her sister.

Marlys' friends, buddies at school, at the little cafe, during the long investigation, now grown and with children of their own. Friends then, and now, through all eternity.

The Compassionate Friends, Inc., especially to the Valley Forge, Pennsylvania, Chapter who helped me say 'Marlys' out loud and let me cry without saying 'don't cry,' and to the Delaware County, Pennsylvania, Chapter where I found the inspiration for this book.

My Story

Years ago when I started working with and writing for grieving parents, I felt I had to establish my credentials as a bereaved mother. I had to talk about my daughter's murder. I had to say her name, Marlys Ann Wohlenhaus, hoping people would remember her. I had to tell how I found her, even had to summarize how the investigation was proceeding. I needed to verbalize what happened to her because her death had become my story.

I am different now, which is why I have my own story. Mine is one of healing and hope, of memories that comfort, of butterflies, angels and roses. Though I will always miss Marlys, I have her with me now as an integral part of my being. I live a good life, filled with love for and from my lovely surviving children, and their children. Jack is with me, my husband and partner, and his lovely children and their children help make us happy. Life for any mourner is difficult, especially at first, but it can also be good in time. Different but good. This book will show you the road toward healing and the paths I took on my journey.

Frances Wohlenhaus-Munday
May, 2003
Casa Mariposa
Isanti County, Minnesota

for
Marlys Ann Wohlenhaus
January 11, 1961 — May 10, 1979

Prologue

GRANNY SAID,
a short history

Someone was ripping away at history, tearing at my place of stories, my land of happy and sad memories. The old ivy covered tree still stood at the edge of the property like I remembered it from my childhood. Now years later, an adult with my own children, I approached the land and still had the excitement of a child. I had visited this place many times with my Granny. This was the place where I had stood often listening to Granny tell me of the events that shaped her life near the turn of the century. Granny's favorite story was that her mother had sewn a button on General Lee's jacket when his Confederate troops were in the area during the battle of Five Forks. General Lee and his men had taken refuge in the area and her house was the home he used. They were heading to Appomattox not many miles away where General Lee and his troops surrendered.

This time, however, there was something shocking before my eyes. The property never had bulldozers before. The land wasn't at all like it was when I was 9 years old, listening to Granny tell me stories about her life as a young girl, living in the house where she was raised. So often when we came there, she described the many fireplaces, one in every bedroom, plus in the living room and kitchen. She told me about the house that had been destroyed by fire, before my memory really. When I came here with her, I could imagine the house from Granny's description, like when she pointed out the space where the house once stood, framed by the tall chimneys at each end. Framed also by the tall ivy covered oak trees.

Granny and I would stand near the old home place. She would tell the story, pointing in the direction of the woods behind the chimneys. "Over there," she would say as she lifted her hand and pointed toward the trees. She would swallow hard and say, "My father, Benjamin and my brothers Henry and George and two sisters, Nealy Frances and Betsy Jane are buried back there". Her voice painted vivid pictures for me as she told the story of those tragic deaths so many years past. "A long time ago" she would say, "there was a narrow lane leading up along the fence line over there. It's lost in a cluster of trees now." She showed me where the fence divided the property from the neighbor who had his pasture on the other side. A wealthy man with lots of land and cattle, he was a kind neighbor. "The graves are actually on the property this man owned," Granny would say to me. "He had been very nice to us during that awful time and told us that our family was welcome to use whatever we needed to bury the family. He even cut down some of his trees so we could build pine boxes for our dead."

I shuddered every time I heard about the merciless diphtheria epidemic that had struck the area, taking first one family and then another. Granny's family was stricken in turn. The whole family was exposed to the disease. Her father was the first to die. When each child became sick, the healthy ones would bathe and dress them in their Sunday clothes. It was uncertain that anyone could survive the sickness, and the task of preparing the dead for burial would have been much harder than doing so ahead of time. Who would be next? Granny already wore her Sunday dress and waited to die. During the next week two more children died but Granny managed to become stronger, somehow having the strength to fight the sickness in herself and then helping the family cope with taking care of each other. It was quite a task for a ten year old. Her father and four siblings did not survive, but she struggled on, learning a way of living that would always be with her. Years later, Granny would choose to be a mid-wife and nurse. Granny wanted to care for others.

Many times on our visits to the old home place, Granny would promise that some day she and I would take a walk in those woods to look for the graves together. Where the trees stood now had been an open field in 1893. The path that led back behind the house was no longer visible after a huge patch of blackberry bushes took over. Maybe it was because it would be hard to walk in the woods through the bramble bushes that we postponed our exploring, but someday we planned to go on that walk. Granny told me the graves were not marked with regular tombstones because their family was poor and could not afford markers. The surviving children had gathered field stones, marking each grave individually.

Now with the bulldozers on this property, I realized that my chance of finding the graves had disappeared. Out of nowhere, a housing development had been planted right in the middle of the trees that my Granny had pointed to so many times in the past. "Over there," she would say, and now over there were houses.

I drove further into the new development, feeling a rush of anger mixed with pain that filled my soul. Would it be too late? How many times I had thought of going on that walk with Granny, before Granny died in May 1960. Oh so many times I had thought about taking the time to go look for those graves. Now I felt the pain of 'if only'. "Why did I wait so long?" I cried to Mom.

The new houses were in various stages of construction but no one was living in the development yet. It had been planned carefully, with cul-de-sacs and bending roads weaving throughout the woods dominated by giant oak and pine trees. Driving on the winding streets gave me a feeling that there was something sacred here. I felt I was rushing headlong toward this hallowed ground. We had no idea where we would even begin to look. The paths that may have been marked by the old fence were gone amid the excavation and clearing as they proceeded to shape the property for the houses.

Mom and I were searching as we drove along. We decided to walk up the banks of earth and into the woods, hoping desperately for a sign of the graves. We had very little time because the sun was starting to cast shadows as it settled behind those beautiful trees. It would be dark soon. We got out of the car and hurried to see what we could find. We went in different directions, staying close to the road in sight of the car and each other. I walked hurriedly away from Mom, up one bank of bulldozed earth and then another, between drainage ditches. I frantically looked for any rocks that might be piled up. I was hoping to see at least one rock, any rock that might lead me to the graves. Mom was walking on the roadway because it was difficult for her to go up and down the dirt banks and drainage ditches. We called to each other on several occasions to be sure each other was all right.

Then I heard a frantic cry. "Frances," Mom yelled, "come quick." I went running toward her.

I was sure that she had found a sign, maybe a rock that marked the graves. When I reached Mom, tears were streaming down her face. "What happened?" I gasped.

"It was Mama, I heard my Mama's voice. She said, 'They're right here.'" My Mother had heard the voice of her mother, my Granny, telling her

5

that she was near the graves. Could this be? Had she really communicated beyond the grave? Had Mom heard the voice of someone who had died more than twenty years before?

By now it was too dark to look any further. We quickly jotted down the names and phone numbers of the developers, planning to call them and tell them about the graves. When we reached Mom's house, I rushed to the phone, only to find that the offices were closed. It was now after 7:00 P.M. I left messages on both numbers letting them know the urgency. Time went slowly now while we waited for a call.

The next day was Saturday, a beautiful day, sunny and bright without a cloud in the sky. Mom and I were anxious for the phone to ring and at 9:00 A.M. the developer returned our call. "Yes", he said, "I know about the graves. We had to stop construction because we found a burial site beside one of the houses. We are not able to continue building until we find who is buried there. We have someone checking with the County of Chesterfield trying to find out who owned that property." He offered to meet us at the property to show us where the graves were.

"Yes, yes," I said. "We'll be there in half an hour."

We could not contain ourselves. The suspense was really getting to Mom and me. Where were those graves? Were we really in the right area? Was it near where Mom had said that she heard Granny's voice? All of these questions were going over and over in our minds and we were talking with excitement now. This man might really know where the graves are.

We drove up to the old home place one more time. Excitement once again filled my heart. I also felt hope with the possibility that someone could show us the place in our history where Granny grew up and almost died.

We met the man who had called us that morning. "The graves are over here," he said. "Follow me. They're right over here."

When we approached one of the homes not yet completed, we were amazed to find it to be the very same house that Mom stood in front of yesterday at nightfall. Mom had been on the road approximately 25 feet away from the graves. When we came to the actual burial site we saw that the graves were not marked anymore. Time had eroded away the granite field stones that had been so tearfully piled on the graves those many years ago. All that was visible were the sunken spots and small fist size rocks over the ground where the pine boxes had been buried.

"What do we do now?" I asked. "We can't leave these graves here so close to this house, I said. They will be trampled on. Besides," I argued, "the buyers may not want graves in their yard."

The developer began to explain the procedure used in moving graves. We listened carefully. We had so much to do now and it wasn't a simple task. He told us that all known living relatives had to be contacted so that they could be a part of this transfer of the burial site. This part of the history of our family would be preserved just as the telling of the story had been kept alive all these years by my Granny and then by my memory. The procedure was good as well as important. This was a special time —a time of remembering, a time of being part of the past in a very special way. The proper authorities were notified and necessary paper work filled out. Grandfather Benjamin Watkins had fought in the Civil War, making this yet another part of history that was special to us. That too needed to be part of the re-interment.

Granny was a very strong, hard working person and yet she always found time to pass on traditions that she thought would be good for me to know and pass on. History like this had been one such important part of her life which she wanted to be a part of mine. Loving, being kind to her neighbors, passing on traditions, keeping events alive or maybe even making history was all part of the way Granny lived. Now, from heaven, she still played a role in that history.

Just down the road from Granny's old home place was an intersection called "Five Forks." To history buffs, Five Forks is well known as the site of one of the major battles in the Civil War. There is a public cemetery nearby, where I often visited the graves of other gone but remembered relatives. Now I could visit this cemetery again, to bury my Great Grandfather Watkins and four of his children. A common grave marked with a bronze plaque, their resting place would be marked for the first time. Now others will know they lived. Mom and I will have a place to go now, remembering always the words of Granny that will ever be present in our thoughts. "They are over there," she would say —even from beyond the grave. Granny knew the importance of remembering. Those you love are just as close as a memory away. My Granny said!

* * * *

In 1960, Granny moved in with my mother in Chesterfield County, Virginia. She very sick with cancer, needed care. She grew weaker and weaker but refused to go to the hospital until I arrived from Minnesota with my son Ray, her great grandson. I was pregnant with Marlys on May 14, 1960 the day my Granny died, but I did not know that at the time. My Granny's determination was sad and wonderful, passing on one generation to the next, remembering back in time.

Now, as you will see from the rest of this book, my life is different, radically different. While Ray and Lynn and their children continue my family's generations and our history, Marlys is missing. She is with Granny.

1

A Place In The Country

Long ago I lived in the country —space dear to my heart, where I walked in the woods, picked wild flowers, wild fruits and enjoyed the smell of clean fresh air.

I grew up that way in Chesterfield County, Virginia, and when I married, I was thrilled to be able to live in the country with my children. Afton, Minnesota is a tiny village, hardly worthy of the name town. When I first moved there with my son Ray, born in 1959, my daughters Marlys, born in 1961, and Lynn born in 1963, Afton had a Post Office, a barber shop, a country store, an ice house and an old hotel. I felt happiness giving my children some of the same things I had grown up with. I felt lucky to be in Afton where I shared my love of nature, watched wild animals in the yard from the picture window of our home, hunted for agates (rocks that had been beautifully designed by nature many millions of years ago). I often said it was easier for the children to find the agates because the young ones were closer to the ground, but I too enjoyed the hunt for these beautiful treasures.

Living on just over 13 acres, we had the best that nature could offer. Trails lead up the hill behind the house to fields of wildflowers, wild asparagus growing everywhere, an apple orchard, wild plum trees, berry bushes —you name it. There were paths below the house where a deep gully supplied wild orchids, mushrooms, ferns. The variety of nature made it so much fun to go for walks. The woods were filled with wild life. Many times we would see a fox on the clearing or deer would come at nightfall and graze on the fragile undergrowth that nourished them throughout the year. Paradise, I thought as I treasured this country life.

May 8, 1979 changed my outlook on life. When I drove to this sanctuary we called home that fateful day, I was not prepared for what I would find when I went inside. My older daughter Marlys Ann Wohlenhaus lay beaten to death in our home. I left, never to return. The country no longer was a place where I would feel safe. Years later, when my husband, Jack, and I would drive in the country, I would say how much I missed the beautiful pines, the white birch trees and the wildlife. But more than that, I missed Marlys and being in the country not only gave me fear, but brought me pain knowing that there was where she was killed.

An unsolved murder has so much baggage, such as not knowing who or what to be afraid of. I had run away; was hiding in places that were different now —places where neighbors were close by and could watch out for each other. I felt like I was in exile. How long would my fear hold me prisoner?

In 1998, an evil man, Joseph Donald Ture, Jr. was sentenced to life in prison for first degree homicide in murdering my daughter Marlys. This sentence would begin after he served a similar term for killing his last victim. Finally I had some reassurance that this serial killer would be locked up for a long time. Then on May 10, 1999 (the twentieth anniversary of Marlys' death) he was indicted for killing 4 more people. Now, no parole board in its right mind would ever let him out. Security of that knowledge lifted fear from my soul —no more was I being held hostage. What a relief to finally be free when I went into the country. What a good feeling!

Jack and I had talked many times about my fears and how now, at long last, I had overcome many of those moments of terror. We now had answers to who murdered Marlys and why he did so. We even began talking about property on a lake somewhere —a dream perhaps, but never-the-less, we could now consider something different from where we have lived for the past twenty plus years.

Christmas of 1999, we were back in Minnesota to celebrate with my two surviving children and some of our grandchildren. We called it "Christmas with the Midwest family." We would have "Christmas with the East Coast family" when we returned to Pennsylvania. In Minnesota, we drove around a lake looking at places that were for sale, some boarded up for the winter, some were lived in 'year round.' There were not many properties for sale. Who goes looking for lake cottages with snow on the ground? Well, we did and sure enough, we ended up on a dead end road where a "For Sale Sign" was hanging. When we called the number on the flyer, of course we surprised the broker who was in another town about twenty miles away not expecting someone to be out looking at property in the snow. Was this a place where I could live? It sure was country!

When we finalized the deal on the house at the lake, I felt so uplifted by knowing that I could walk down a wooded path, collect wild berries, fruits and ornamental items for crafts and even sit and watch wildlife in my own yard. Gone was that griping pain and fear. I could remember the times I took my three children on walks and I could also have that same special time with my grandchildren —precious time because fear no longer imprisoned me. Being near my children and enjoying their laughter on a regular basis is truly a gift. That treasured country setting was given to me by my loving husband Jack who tried to understand the person he married after the death of her daughter. In doing so, he also came to understand who I really am deep down inside. He knows that my children are my closest connection to Marlys who they miss as much as I do. When we are together, Marlys is there also because her spirit lives with us for all eternity.

As Jack and I draw closer to the golden years of our life together, our eyes see with different meaning. We need special time with family and with friends, but we also need time to reflect on the past —as it used to be, life as it is today and life as we hope it will be in the future. Ours is a future of hopes and dreams of a good life, not a life of luxury but of happiness and joy. Joy comes from dreaming dreams and then following where those visions lead. A house by the lake, a private get-a-way, a sanctuary for rest and relaxation as we remember what we have lost, but most of all treasure what we have. Love can never be taken away and certainly we don't want to ever stop dreaming.

She's Not Your Daughter

"She wasn't your daughter," I cried. "How do you know how I feel?"

Many times, I lashed out at Jack with hurting words like these. Once more, he just wanted to know that I would be okay. He needed to be part of my life, to help me through this terrible pain. But my agony was too great and I didn't think anyone could know how to help me cope. It seemed like everyone wanted my pain to go away. Even Jack was trying to make me feel better. But how could I ever feel better again in my life with all the horrible memories of finding Marlys

14

murdered in my home? My life would never be the same. My pain was real, not simply something to get over.

During the first few years after the murder, every time I tried to answer a question about my daughter, I would cry. Every time I thought about Marlys I would cry. I was reaching a point that all I did, it seemed, was cry. I shed tears in church, at the supermarket, it really didn't matter where I was, I would just start to weep. I did not know how I would ever reach a point where I would be able to say Marlys again without breaking up. Whenever I started to say her name, all my well meaning friends and loved ones would say, "Oh don't cry, it will be okay." I knew it would never be okay, but they didn't.

When I found the Valley Forge, Pennsylvania, chapter of The Compassionate Friends, I was finally was able to say Marlys with tears streaming down my checks and no one said "don't cry." I finally felt free. Tears are healing for the soul and when our child dies, our very soul really does need healing. I soon realized that Jack was also hurting. He was not Marlys' biological father, but he would miss her from day to day. He too felt an emptiness. After all, they were good friends and now he no longer could see her sweet smile and hear her laughter. This is pain too. Maybe not the same as mine, because we all grieve differently, but certainly Jack was mourning too. Letting him share in the memories and feel my emotions has helped me to understand many aspects of grief and healing. Jack will tell you that living with me

15

for all these years has not always been easy, but sharing the pain as well as the joys is the only way to survive this overwhelming tragedy that has devastated our lives.

When, finally, we pick up the pieces and start to recognize that others are present, we see a butterfly, feel the softness of an angel's wing or smell the sweetness of a rose —maybe for just a moment our child has visited us with a reminder of their love that is ever present. We remember step-parents, siblings and grandparents grieve too. We share the love and share the memories.

Springtime Again

How can it be Springtime again? My child is not with me and yet Spring comes anyway. The month of May will always be a time of sadness for me, yet it is such a beautiful month. I look around and see all the beautiful flowering shrubs, budding trees, blooming plants, new life bursting forth everywhere. I wish that just for a moment I could turn to Marlys and say, "Look at this!" But I can't do that.

I must try very hard to see the beauty of Spring. The sun is warm again. Happiness is everywhere, butterflies fluttering by, birds chirping and flying about. In my heart Marlys is sharing that beauty with me everyday. I just didn't know it for a while.

It takes a long time to understand I will never lose my child, nor how I feel about her. Marlys will always be in my heart —as close as the whisper of a gentle Spring breeze. My memories take me on that garden path, stopping to smell the roses, picking the delicate violet, feeling the touch of the butterfly, soft as an angel's wing. I will try to fill Springtime with beauty —the beauty of memories of my beloved daughter.

Dancing With Daises

Our home in Afton, built in 1968 and where I raised my three children, sat on a slight grade leading up a hill. The front yard was as large and as flat as a football field but the back yard had to be terraced with sod because it was pretty steep. Without the grassy lawn meandering gently down the hill, there would have been mud slides every time it rained. The kennels for my Saint Bernards and the barn for the horses were at the top of the hill. This let me see a beautiful setting out my kitchen window. The Saints would romp and play and I could see the horses graze. Of course there were always one or two Saint Bernards in the house to keep me company.

The beautiful natural grassy field beyond the kennel and barn stretched for acres. Often my children and I would go for walks in early Spring, looking for asparagus, dandelion greens and winter cress which was abundant from April until the early part of June. I would get teased by Ray, Marlys and Lynn about collecting "weeds" to eat. I enjoyed the fresh greens and especially the asparagus just as it popped from the ground. I truly enjoyed having my children with me to experience nature and enjoy this beauty. From the top of that hill, we could see the Northern States Power company tower in Bayport approximately twelve miles away. It was awesome, like standing on top of the world.

When Summer came, wild flowers completely covered the top of the hill. This area had not been disturbed except for pheasants and deer we often saw when we walked along our path to gather our treasures. We knew the flowers popped up for us to gather and enjoy in our home. Daisies were everywhere and oh so beautiful as they danced in the gentle breeze of Summer.

After Marlys died, I no longer had an opportunity to walk along those paths. Because her murder had taken place in our home, I chose to never go back there to live. I packed up what I needed from the house several months after her death, no longer capable of enduring the pain of entering the house where I found Marlys dying on that horrible Tuesday in May.

Approximately two years after Marlys' death, she came to me in a dream. She was dressed in the blue dress that she was buried in and was smiling and waving from the top of the hill behind the house she grew up in. She was surrounded by daisies that nodded their heads in the wind. Marlys danced and twirled around with a happy look on her face, a radiance I remember from the times when she was with me gathering daisies and teasing me about gathering "weeds."

Yes, Marlys was dancing with daisies surrounding her, smiling and letting me know that she is okay. Dancing on top of the hill that brought so much pleasure when she was growing up —the hill where we shared special time together. Dancing with daises. Marlys is forever with me in thought and yes, forever in my heart.

2

A Rose Garden

A number of years ago, a friend of mine and I had an idea to plant a rose garden at a nearby church as a memorial to those who have had a child die. The rose bush would be planted by an individual if she or he wanted to plant it or we would plant the fragrant flower for them. The roses would be carefully selected and there would be many colors in the area by the steps leading up to the church, a welcome for all to see when they arrived for the Sunday services. There are not many gardens more beautiful than a rose garden.

I purchased three rose bushes to plant in memory of Marlys. The ground had been prepared, holes dug and the watering hose lay ready nearby. The plants were budding enough to let me see hints of the beautiful colors. Excitement filled the air, anticipating what the blossoms would look like in the months ahead.

Just at the time when I bent down to place a rose bush in the ground, a butterfly flew around me and landed on the rose. I was in awe at seeing the butterfly and I felt I had a sign from Marlys. I looked up to see a friend of mine coming down the steps. Nellie had been a member of the church for a long time, and her daughter had died the previous year. Nellie asked why I was planting the bushes. I told her they were in memory of Marlys and she could plant some in memory of her daughter, Susan also. Tears welled in Nellie's eyes, then she said she was not able to do work like that. She wished she could plant one in memory of Susan. While I continued to put the dirt in around the roots, I told Nellie that I would be happy to help her plant a bush for Susan.

When I was finished planting my roses, I told Nellie I would drive her to the garden center so she could pick out her roses. Then we'd come back to the church to plant them. The garden center was just a few miles away, so we were back in no time.

It did not take long to prepare the holes for Nellie's bushes and when she and I were placing the plants in the soil, two butterflies circled around us and went to the flowers in front of us. We could not believe our eyes. I had told Nellie of the butterfly I had seen earlier when I planted Marlys' bush, but now there were two beautiful Swallowtails, bright yellow and black —one for Marlys and one for Susan. Were they little visitors, signs that our children are okay in a new life? We definitely felt their presence when the butterflies fluttered around us.

Whatever the butterflies meant on that day, it was a spirit filled moment for two mothers, reaching out to each other, helping in a simple way to bring beauty to a sacred space in memory of two daughters whose lives ended way too soon. There was comfort in finding the butterflies.

A Solitary Rose

A rose is one of the most beautiful flowers, with a fragrance that lingers on my mind for a long time after I have stopped to smell them. I keep bowls of rose petals around the house, refreshing these petals with pure essence of rose oil from time to time. The petals for the most part are those I have collected from my rose gardens over the years. One rose stands out above all the others.

Jack and I go to Mexico the first two weeks of each year to enjoy the sunny Caribbean weather in our time share Villa. Both weeks are on the beach, but since we don't have the weeks in the same unit, we have to move to the second one. The weeks go from Saturday to Saturday and New Years week-end does not count, so we are always in Cancun on January 11th, Marlys' Birthday.

This year, after over twenty years, Jack and I both commented that Marlys' birthday this year seemed emptier than most. I felt sad and tears were ready to flow while we continued eating breakfast on the patio. Once again, we wished that Marlys could have grown up, married and had children like her sister Lynn. They could have come to Cancun like Lynn's daughter Melanie, who had spent that first week enjoying the beach, sun and visiting the sites in the surrounding area. And yes, visiting us at our Villa.

While Jack and I packed our belongings and waited to move to our second week Villa, I felt okay but still that sadness of Marlys' death remained with me. Why this time on her birthday? I thought I was fine —there had been so many years of birthdays and anniversaries after her death.

On arriving at the second Villa, my eyes went directly to the divider between the kitchen and dining area. There in a water bottle was a long stemmed pure white rose. The fragrance was awesome. The sweetness and beauty of a rose. Who put it there and why on this day? We never did find out who gave us this treasure. Was it an angel? Tears filled my eyes —tears of sadness and tears of joy. Was this a little sign of the sweetness of Marlys' life while she was physically with us? I think so. A rose is a reminder of delicate beauty and Marlys was certainly with us that day. A solitary rose —the petals will be put with the other petals that delight us where we enjoy their fragrance in our home.

Plant A Butterfly Garden

Springtime is such a beautiful time of the year. Everything is fresh and new as the old leaves are pushed away to make way for the fresh green buds. New growth appears on the trees and shrubs. New life, new beginnings and here comes the new season for planning a butterfly garden.

Where do I begin? Some people have a nice large yard, some only have a small space, while others have no space for a garden. That does not worry the butterfly —they know we will plan for them. And so we begin.

People who have a large yard will be able to plant flowering shrubs, butterfly bushes, and other exciting and enticing plants to attract the little friends who flutter around looking for nectar. The small yards will need to be planned more carefully but still there will be space for some of the butterfly's favorites. For those who have no space —perhaps only a patio or door step, they can fill a large pot with the butterfly's favorite flowers. And yes, they will come.

A pot filled with my favorite herbs will make the butterflies very happy. Basil, Dill, Mint, Sage and Thyme will attract my little friends. The list goes on to flowers: Ageratum, Cosmos, Viola, Candytuft, Nasturtium, Sweet Alyssum, Zinnia, Pinks, Marigold, Phlox, Forget-Me-Not, Aster, Lavender, Lupine, Mallow, Sunflowers, Sweet William and Verbena. Take your pick, plan your garden, large or small.

The butterfly has a life cycle that includes the stage of being a leaf-eating caterpillar as well as being a free-flying adult butterfly. There must be food nearby for both stages. Do not worry about the flowers —because the larvae of many species of butterflies prefer to feed on weeds, and even if they feast on some of our flowers, we only need to grow a few more plants. The risk of losing a plant to a butterfly is really very small.

Butterflies need sun and, since their wings are delicate, also need protection, so sheltered garden areas are preferred. Butterflies also need water to drink and cannot drink from open water such as a bird-bath. A small basin buried in the soil and filled with sand, dirt and water will furnish just the right amount of moisture to encourage the butterfly and take care of its water needs.

There are lots of different varieties of butterflies to look for in my area so I will keep my eyes open and watch for the signs of Spring —butterflies darting here and there enjoying new life and the beauty of sunshine and flowers. I will select a few of the above flowers and herbs and watch as my little friends gather to enjoy the delicious beauty of my garden. I will notice their delicate grace when they land on a flower for a moment, then flutter skyward.

The Painted Lady

Jack and I lived in Ocean City, Maryland, back in the early 1990s in a townhouse on the Bay. An open field adjoined the townhouse, where I could walk my dog and tend the flowers. I had planted flowers and shrubs along the entire length of our property. Of course it was cluttered, as Jack would say, with lots of specimens that I had brought with me from our previous homes. My plants have learned to travel well —I pack them in pots with my special soil and take them whenever we move. That particular year I even had cantaloupe, tomatoes and peppers in my flower garden. During the week, Jack worked out of town. He traveled back and forth to Pennsylvania, spending Thursday night until Monday morning home with me at the Bay. So, that left me with spare time to do craft projects with my neighbor friend Jean. She and I had fun collecting sea shells, making them into beautiful objects.

One day I saw an advertisement in a magazine offering caterpillars that one could watch go through their process from larva to butterfly. I couldn't resist. The package arrived complete with a little tent where the larva would attach themselves at the top, spin a cocoon and hang until the right time to be transformed. This process is called chrysalis. I don't remember how long it took, but I recall the thrill of watching these strange little cocoons transform into beautiful Painted Ladies. What a joy to watch them flutter and then try to fly. When they were all out of their cocoon, Chelsea, one of my granddaughters, and I, took the tent outside to my flower garden and carefully opened the tent and waited. The Painted Ladies slowly came out, then immediately found a colorful flower where it drank from its nectar, and then flew away to other flowers.

It's funny, but little Painted Ladies have followed me everywhere it seems. They were the first butterflies of color (white ones seem to be the very first) to come to my garden at the house we called Rosecastle, in Pennsylvania. Then when I went to Minnesota to visit, before we moved back, there to greet me were Painted Ladies —every day, Painted Ladies. I also regularly see other varieties such as the Monarch, the Mormon Metalmark and the Yellow Tiger Swallowtail.

One day, while I worked in the yard in Minnesota, a Painted Lady followed me. She was basking in the warm sunshine, darting from place to place —even stopping to join me on the garage floor when I moved stuff from one stack to another. The Painted Lady. What was she saying to me? Was she reminding me of good times from the past? Was she keeping me ever alert to the fragility of life? Whatever her mission, she brought joy as she fluttered around me. A presence, a reminder that joy does exist.

I spent that Summer in Minnesota, from June until August, while Jack traveled back and forth from there to Rosecastle. I had my butterflies, and so did Jack, as a reminder that we are not alone.

Kissed By Butterflies

Jack and I look forward to our vacation in Mexico every January. It was usually cold, snowy or a time of ice storms when we lived in Pennsylvania —not to mention Minnesota— so we looked forward to getting away. The time we plan for our vacation is a time of relaxation, to reenergize ourselves for the year ahead. 1998 was an extremely stressful year for me, especially with the hearings, trial and final conviction of Marlys' murderer. On top of that I had surgery, from which I healed on schedule.

When Jack and I are on vacation we do some of the same things we do at home, such as sit on the balcony or patio and talk about our children, grandchildren, future plans, etc. The time we spend together like this is very special because we get many new ideas and keep in touch with each other's thoughts. And we always look for butterflies.

One morning soon after we arrived in Mexico, Jack was anxious to tell me about a dream he had. He said Marlys came to him in the dream and was holding his hand. She was writing something in his palm as she sang *We Are Family* —an old song that we have not heard in years. Needless to say, I felt a little envious because I did not have that dream, but I am so happy that he did and was delighted to hear him tell the story. To Jack, this was yet another way that Marlys was affirming that he and I are together and happy.

A few days later we rented a car and went to a popular tourist attraction. We chose XCARET because they have a huge butterfly sanctuary. Jack and I have been to butterfly exhibits in the United States and are always thrilled to see so many varieties. But this place, XCARET, is truly a sanctuary. We walked through caves along crystal clear rivers and finally came to an opening that led us into a beautiful garden complete with stepping stone paths, waterfalls, tropical plants and every beautiful butterfly that we could imagine. As we walked through this "paradise", the butterflies flew around us, darting from one beautiful flower to another. Occasionally a butterfly would land on our clothing and of course we were excited to have them come so close. When we were heading back along the path following the exit signs, I experienced a tremendous joy. I felt the flutter of many butterflies on my shoulders and neck. It thrilled me to feel the delicate touch of these angels of nature. Yes there was joy in the garden filled with butterflies and stepping stones. I had been kissed by the butterflies.

3

Soft Breeze

How often have you felt a soft breeze and instantly your thoughts went floating away to times gone by when your child was beside you? How many times have you actually felt a gentle touch and look to find that you are standing alone in the garden? Could these be gentle realities that our child is still with us, in spirit, no matter how long it has been since she or he died?

I had just such an experience. A person I knew from a support group I attended the night before was upset, not able to listen to the pain of others because her grief was still so fresh. I talked with her that evening and I struggled with what to say that would help her toward her healing. I invited her to my home for coffee the next morning and she agreed to come.

That morning when I woke up, I was still struggling with what I could say and how I should approach her pain. Of course I want to say the right things, but I also want my friend Ann to understand there is a process to healing, and she alone must take the steps in the right direction.

While I waited for her to arrive at my home, I busied myself caring for my plants in the garden, taking off a few dead blossoms, photographing one or two of my prize plants. As I worked, words came to me, *If your child's death destroys your life, then your child's life meant nothing.* I thought, *Those words are pretty straightforward.*

Continuing my little tasks in the garden led me to the fountain in the courtyard. I stood there with the garden hose in my hand filling the fountain and bird bath. Suddenly I felt a gentle breeze and once more the words came to me, *If your child's death destroys your life, then your child's life meant nothing.* I immediately looked up and turned around, this time realizing that those words were coming from Marlys. She gave me a message for my friend who needed encouragement. They were words that would help her cross those rough and rugged stepping stones. Call it inspiration or simply an understanding of the process, but to me, on that morning, those words were heaven sent. A gentle breeze, a little visit, words giving hope as I reached out to another grieving mother.

Angels On The Beach

Some years ago, Jack and I went to Sanibel Island, Florida, for a much needed one week vacation. There had been so many stresses and when our week to Sanibel drew near, we were ready to go.

Jack always takes lots of books to read and, of course, his lap-top computer so he can write for his enjoyment. I was looking forward to searching the shoreline for seashells. Each day I checked the tide chart and planned my day so I could be there for both high and low tides, hoping some fantastic shell would appear in front of me. Every day, I came back to our little apartment with a net full of small but beautiful treasures.

One particular day, I had been seeing many special shells while I walked along the beach. A father and his two little girls, approximately ages 3 and 5, were searching for shells but really didn't know where to look. I guessed it was their first time on the island. When I passed by the family, I noticed that they were watching me as I bent over to pick up shells. At about the same time, a beautiful little whelk shell washed up in front of me. I reached out toward the 5 year old and asked if she would like to have the shell. She was very excited and her father said it was okay. She ran happily to tell her mother about the shell I had given her.

The next day I was back on the beach again but this time I did not see the family. I walked along, surrounded by the warm sun and gentle breeze, almost as if I was being hugged by the heavens. Just then, out of nowhere it seemed, the 5 year old came running up to me. "Here," she said, "this is for you!" I looked at her outstretched hand, and noticed a beautiful little seashell. I said, "Are you sure you want to give that one away?" She reached up and laid the shell in my hand and said again, "This is for you!" Almost before I could get the words "thank you" out of my mouth, she ran away, back to her family, who had not come to the beach yet.

What a special visit! A little stranger on the beach. Or was it? All I know is that a flood of beautiful memories washed over me, reminding me of my children when they were that age and how excited they were when they found a beautiful seashell. Strangers? Special visits? Hugs from Heaven? Angels on the beach? All are mine to have whenever I remember.

Little Visits Even Now

When my children were small we had rabbits and in fact we still had rabbits when Marlys was attacked in our home. Rabbits have always been cuddly and fun to play with.

Several years ago, my granddaughter Nicole gave me a Netherland Dwarf Rabbit. I named him Bertie after my maternal grandfather. Bertie was a sweet bunny and I enjoyed playing with him because he was so tiny and his cage was right outside the back door of the house we were living in while we built our new home. Bertie was lonely however. The wild rabbits that lived nearby would come and tease him, so I decided to get a doe and have little bunnies. That was very easy. A friend of mine had just the perfect purebred doe and we named her Sophía.

Sophía was bred right away and on May 8th she delivered five beautiful little perfectly healthy baby bunnies. There were two females and three males. I decided that I wanted to keep a female and I named her Mayo (Spanish for May). She developed into a beautiful adult and like Sophía, was spoiled rotten because I played with them every day. I found a home for Bertie because he was just a little large for the breed.

Summer passed with lots of fun with the bunnies, but when it started to get cold, I was unable to spend the time with them that I wanted to and thought they deserved. They were happy in their cages and seemed to really enjoy the cold weather, but I felt sorry for them being cooped up without me able to play with them daily.

In the meantime, a friend gave me two half Flemish Giant buck rabbits that needed a home. She said that I could release them in my yard and they would have a good life and still be pets. We named them Salt and Pepper. Soon I got two more and released them. Their names were Sugar (a doe) and Spice (a buck). Salt vanished after about a month. Maybe he found a friend in the wild or something happened to him but the rest of the bunnies constantly hop around the yard.

My granddaughter Nicole had decided she was getting to old for 4-H. Besides, having all those show rabbits she had made for a lot of work. Nicole gave me a purebred Flemish Giant doe and a purebred Mini Lop doe and I released them.

Now the yard had bunnies teasing Sophía and Mayo, who were too small to be released. The more I watched the rabbits running free, the more I felt sorry for my two little ones in the cage.

One of my friends raises rabbits and I decided to see if she knew anyone who might want to purchase Sophía and Mayo. She said she would call me back by the week-end. On Saturday morning the phone rang and it was my friend Angel. She said she had found a lady who would like to come and look at the bunnies. I said they could come out right away if they wanted to.

About a half hour later Angel came with the lady to look at the two Netherlands. The lady who came with Angel was thrilled and said she would take both of them. They would have a wonderful home. She was a rabbit breeder and showed her rabbits around the state. When she came inside to get the papers and pay me for the rabbits, I heard Angel call her by name. Angel said, "Marlys." I said, "Did I here you say your name is Marlys?" She said yes, and smiled. I was shocked. When she left promising to care for my little babies, I was still in disbelief.

I closed the door and went to the library where Jack was sitting and I said to him, "Guess who bought the rabbits?" Then I showed him the check. Marlys was printed on the top of the check. Needless to say, he was stunned. A woman named Marlys had purchased Sophía and my little baby Mayo who was born on May 8th, the day my Marlys was attacked in my home so many years ago. Was this another little visit? Angel had brought Marlys to my home. Memories flooded my heart because I am always looking for a connection to Marlys wherever I can find it. In the sale of two rabbits? Yes, I will never forget and just hearing that beautiful name, Marlys, brings happiness.

Do You See The Wonder?

One of my favorite songs has words that describe how I feel most of the time. Remember I said, most of the time. The song is sung by Nana Mouskari and is entitled, *I Believe In Angels*. The song begins, saying "If you see the wonder in a fairy tale, you can face the future, even if you fail." This is a very positive statement and most of us, in our grief, are not very positive. It takes a long time for us to move to beyond the negative feelings we have. We need to almost be in a fairy tale world to face the future when our child has died. So many of our dreams for our child, our fantasy of a wonderful life for them, have been ripped away by that terrible tragedy. How can I face the future? Even if I have a strong belief, whether through my faith or as part of an imagined fantasy, how can I face the future?

The song continues, saying that, "I believe in angels, something good in everything I see." Well, let's not get carried away! Yes, I do believe in angels, but can I say something good in everything I see? No, not something good in everything. How can there be good in the death of my child?

Early grief and pain is unbearable. I didn't have a clue as to how to get from one moment to the next, much less face the future. Though time heals slowly, hope eventually emerges and my faith resurfaces a little bit at a time. One day, I will think of my daughter and begin to think of angels and something good. The beautiful memories of my beloved child will start to return to me and I will begin to believe again —in God or in fairy tales— in something good.

Eventually, the positive thoughts started to enter my mind and heart, and I saw myself as a new person. I am no longer the same as I was before Marlys died. Yet, I can reach this point of hope again in my life as I walk along my healing journey of grief. At first I wondered, then I faced the future, sometimes I failed —felt I had slipped backwards. But since I believe in angels and in something good, remembering the beauty of my child, I can once again experience the good in all I see because I am reaching out in peace to those who need me now.

Messages From Heaven

Bereaved parents are constantly looking for a "sign" from their child. They want some communication that tells them their child is okay, happy in her new life. Since Marlys is not with me on this earth, I need to know that she is pleased with what I am doing in her memory. Is my daughter nudging me along in my daily life, encouraging me to "be happy" in all that I do? It is normal for parents to look for these signs even after twenty, thirty, forty or even fifty years after our child has died. I want to know that my child is still with me in spirit, always remembered, loved and missed just as much now as in the early days after her death.

Jack and I spent Mother's Day weekend in 1999 with my daughter Lynn and her family and with my son Ray. We were visiting in Minnesota and it was only fitting that we be there because that Mother's Day was the 20th Anniversary of Marlys' death.

The route we took from the airport was a round about way, because we wanted to go to the cemetery where Marlys had originally been buried. Her stone is still there, a place where her brother and sister go and where her friends went as well. We placed roses on the stone, pausing to remember the saddest day of our lives. Driving along the highway we remembered the places that were so precious to all of us at one time. The places that Marlys knew so well —our home town.

It felt like Marlys was leading us on this journey back to Minnesota for Mother's Day. Twenty years is a long time; yet it is also so very short.

Good news greeted us at the Washington County Sheriff's Department when we stopped to see friends there. The day before we arrived, a

Grand Jury had been called in Stearns County, approximately 90 miles from Afton, where Alice Huling and three of her four children had been brutally murdered the December before Marlys was attacked. I felt as if someone was preparing the way for our weekend. The fact that there was a Grand Jury in progress once again gave us a sense of hope with the possibility of justice for yet another family. Was someone helping us deal with the anniversary of Marlys' murder by affirming our work in reaching out to others?

May 10th is, of course, the actual anniversary date of her death and we had scheduled to meet with the Stearns County Attorney over a month ahead of time to encourage him to call the Grand Jury. Now Jack and I were in his office. He told us he was sworn to secrecy and couldn't tell us that such a proceeding is ready to go to deliberation —not even confirm that there was one going on. We felt confident because we knew about the Grand Jury anyway. The news had been leaked by someone and it was on the local radio. But we couldn't get any information out of this person. He would not tell us anything.

Another family, who is still seeking justice for the deaths of their two daughters by murder in 1974, graciously invited us for lunch at their home. It was a friendship that formed because we are fellow travelers in grief. These were friends formed through tragedy. Yet we were one in spirit as we sat together and shared that common bond.

The mother, Rita, had written a beautiful song in memory of her girls, Mary and Susan. She sang it for us after lunch. On the table she had placed a candle, burning in memory of Marlys. She also put a picture drawn by one of her girls on the table, making this a sacred and very special time together. When we looked out the patio door, we saw a pair of Gold Finches. Rita said she had never seen these birds before at their house. How beautiful they were, quietly sitting on the deck, so brightly colored and beautiful. Then they flew away. Was this another a sign for us? Rita and Fred think so. Two hours later the Grand Jury in Stearns County came back with four First Degree Murder Indictments for the murders of Alice and her three children, against the man who killed Marlys. The Huling family waited even longer than we did for justice. We believe in signs, we believe in miracles and we believe in messages from Heaven.

4

Summer - A Rough Time

In talking with many bereaved parents, I have heard them say that Summer can be a rough time. Dealing with vacations, graduations, family gatherings and so on bring up memories, and also bring back some of the pain we experienced because we are reminded of that our child is gone.

One Summer also brought renewed hope to our family. During that time it became quite possible that the person who murdered Marlys would be identified. The law enforcement agencies in Minnesota began a major effort to solve our case, raised the reward, held press conferences, and followed up on leads. At one press conference, the lead officer said that, "We have to make it seem like the murder was committed yesterday, so it will be fresh in everyone's minds." While that may be painful, the possibility of justice has been so important to me and has carried me along. That is the message of helping each other in our bereavement, that there will be comfort for everyone.

One special source of hope was that the national media had become involved. Along with investigators and potential witnesses, I was interviewed, able to make my plea for justice for Marlys. I eagerly looked forward to the CBS television show *48 Hours* on September 12, 1996. They featured our case as a result of all the new publicity.

That Summer has been a reminder of how important the work support groups are in the grieving process. I didn't have such an opportunity in 1979, and I had a much harder time than I would have if others had been around to help. These many years later, I am grateful to all my friends and family who reached out to me —understanding that the pain has resurfaced with almost the same intensity as when Marlys was struck down.

The Hearings

Once our case became active, entered the court system, friends have asked me why I travel to Minnesota for each and every evidence hearing on matters related to the person indicted for murdering Marlys. Most people understand why I would want to be present at the actual trial, but the hearings I have been attending are concerned with crimes against others. The sessions are not pleasant, but I feel compelled to be there for the testimony of every witness.

I have worked for over nineteen years to keep Marlys' memory alive in Minnesota so that she would not be forgotten by Law Enforcement Officials. I needed justice to be done. Marlys is with me always in spirit and her memories have helped me in the healing process while I have struggled to find answers to why she was so brutally attacked. My grief work brings me in contact with so many murder victim families. Because I reach out to them to give hope, I am better equipped to help others with their grief and in doing so, I am helping myself. What I do to accompany others is done in memory of Marlys.

For many years I didn't know who to suspect, but since December, 1996, with the indictment of Joseph Donald Ture, Jr., I have had a realization that the evil one who killed Marlys had killed before, and after. I could not allow any more families to be torn apart by this serial murderer. I would not want this man out of jail, able to kill again. If he is guilty of what he's been accused of doing, he would be a very real risk to others if he was released.

The court time in Stillwater, Minnesota, in April and in June has helped me to understand there are so many victims who had not had a fair day in court. I have been supporting them in their healing process, especially since they can now focus on the perpetrator. I heard seven women testify, then point to Joseph Donald Ture, Jr. and say "this is the person" who sexually assaulted them. They were able to confront him, say, "He did this to me." Marlys and the other murder victims cannot do that. While my support system at home did not deal with rape and other tragic matters where the victim survives, the compassion I learned at the meetings compelled me to reach out to these women as well.

I heard testimony of witnesses who have tied Joe Ture —in our minds— to the murders of Joan Bierschbach and to Alice Huling, her two daughters Susie and Patti, and her son, Wayne. I heard evidence only the murderer would know. I also met the parents of Diane Edwards, of whose murder Joe Ture had been convicted in 1981. All of these families share the tragedy of the death of a child with me. We also have the identity of the perpetrator of these murders in common. Each day the courtroom becomes my bereavement sharing session. Each family member offers and receives comfort; every one understands how I feel. In the court house, I am not alone.

Dreams

Many people wish, even pray, to have at least one dream of their child who has died. A popular program at bereavement support group meetings is the topic of dreams. We listen to motivational tapes, and occasionally have workshops on how to learn to dream of our loved one. When we have such a dream, we count them as small visits from beyond. For some, these messages we receive while we are asleep are very peaceful and joyous; others tell of being very sad after their experience.

I have had a number of dreams of Marlys —all very brief— and usually some type of message has been linked to the dream. Not long after Marlys died, I dreamed of her telling me "I'm okay, Mom." She was safe in the next world, united with my other deceased relatives including my father, Granny and my other grandparents.

When I faced hearings in Minnesota before the trial of the man indicted for murdering Marlys, Jack and I purchased a motor home to live in during that time period, and we prepared for a trip to attend the last of the hearings beginning on August 3, 1998. I had owned a motor home back in the '70's and had traveled in it many times with my children. This seemed like the best solution for all our logistical problems.

I tried to think of everything I might need when I outfitted the motor home for the trip to Minnesota. Jack and I put our clothes in the closet, packed food in the cupboards, refrigerator and freezer, and generally busied ourselves with getting the vehicle ready to leave early the next morning. I stored the assorted items, dishes, pans, and so on. While I stood in the kitchen area, my thoughts went to the times I had traveled with my children. I wished I could show this big RV to Marlys. Ray stopped by to see it earlier in the day and Lynn and her family would see it when I arrived in Minnesota.

Casual thoughts came to me about our reasons for buying this thing —the up-coming trial which was expected to last 2 to 3 months. I wondered what Marlys would think about what I have done so far to solve her murder. I think she would be proud of the work I have done. I'm sure she's proud that I will again be doing everything I can to keep the killer from killing again. When we turned out the lights and went into the house for the night, I felt excitement about the adventure to the midwest. I looked forward to sharing the driving with Jack, to cooking in my mini-kitchen and, truthfully, getting this last week of hearings over with. I had said in conversation with some of our friends who had come by to wish us "god speed" that this whole ordeal was starting to wear on me.

Since I have no trouble sleeping when I am tired, off I went to dreamland. During that peaceful sleep, Marlys came to me, as real as I have ever seen her, so much like she was as a young teen, bubbling with laughter. In the dream, I stood in my mini-kitchen in the motor home and when I looked toward the large window, I saw Marlys standing on what appeared to be the vehicle's bumper. She looked in the window, waved to me, smiling the biggest smile I have ever seen. In my dream I saw a smile and a wave from a very happy girl giving approval to her Mom for what she was doing to, hopefully, bring justice. Then the scene changed. Now Marlys was standing with her sister Lynn and their grandfather —Grandpa Dave— and again Marlys was waving with a happy smile.

When I awoke, I remembered every detail of my dream and I cherish the joy of her little visit. Was that visit giving me a sign I am doing the right thing? I think so. Dreams are messages, some people say. I am so thankful for that vision —that visit, with her smile that said, "Mom, be happy."

Four days after my dream, on August 2, 1998, Grandpa Dave passed away, at the age of 77. Because my daughter Lynn often visited him in the nursing home, I like to think that Marlys was taking him from Lynn, to continue the love.

Camping

In a peaceful, quiet, and beautiful area, surrounded by evergreens, Jack and I set up camp in our motor home we purchased in order to go through the trial that we had hoped would bring justice and peace to our family after over nineteen years. The Minnesota weather had even welcomed us with temperatures far above normal for the Fall of the year. Just to be safe, we did go prepared for colder weather, putting the snow boots and heavy coats in a box packed away, out of sight just in case we needed them.

I was prepared for the weather, and I thought I was also ready for the trial. I had anticipated that the trial would be painful and long, and I also knew that the defense would become ugly

47

sometimes as they did their work to give the defendant a fair trial. I was not however prepared to find out the truth of how the murderer so viciously and brutally continued to strike Marlys after she was already down. Such a petite body, no threat to anyone, attacked by a mad person because she would not have anything to do with him. So much of the explicit details of Marlys' murder had been kept from me because Law Enforcement was preserving what little evidence they had.

The details unraveled and I came to understand that real evil does exist in our world, not only on the cold streets of the big city ghettos, but it lurks in the beautiful suburbs waiting for that innocent, pretty little girl to be caught off guard. We hear on TV more times than we should, about innocent children becoming victims of people who they trust —neighbors or friends. That is scary! In Marlys' case, it was a person who she feared —a person who had been stalking her, following her from school, work or when she was simply having fun with her friends. How can we tell our children and young adults that evil does exist OUT THERE? How can we prepare them for the worst without scaring them, having them paranoid and living in fear? The truth is, we can't.

Once more I was faced with the "if only's", or "what if's." They do surface from time to time and are part of the unresolved baggage that I was carrying when murder entered my life. Knowing in my heart and mind that if I could have changed things, I would have, is not a comfort. There is no doubt about that. But the baggage caught me off guard and sent me once again into the pain of grief. Facing reality and dealing with it as it comes up is so important to the healing process. Sometimes, facing evil has to be done.

The Very Worst

So often I have told people that the death of a child is the worst thing that can happen to a person, and that is true. I like to add more, saying that each type of death comes with its own unique baggage. Well, during the trial in 1998, I found out what it really meant to deal with baggage.

In my own way, I thought I understood that dealing with murder meant facing the fear connected with murder, the unknown in our case, the horror, law enforcement, the justice system, and so on. But little did I know until April 1998, almost nineteen years after the homicide that took Marlys from me, what it was really like to face the one who murdered Marlys, every day for weeks on end.

When the trial began in September of that year, I had to relive the events of May 8, 1979 over and over when each witness took the stand, some to explain how the murderer had bragged to them about what he had done. I learned how this perpetrator thought he was going to get away with his crime because it happened so long ago. Each day as I sat in court, the murderer sipped his glass of water and laughed and talked with his Defense Attorneys, seemingly enjoying his temporary freedom away from his jail cell. I as a victim was not allowed any food or drink in the courtroom. During the testimony, very large autopsy photos of Marlys and other victims were held up for all to see. The defendant looked at them as though they were trophies. I only glanced at the photos and stared at the killer with disgust. Why should he be allowed to see Marlys or the other victims? Step by step I saw the evidence —awful, unbelievable baggage.

The Jury seemed to hang on every word and when the Prosecution gave a two hour and twenty-seven minute closing statement, I could have heard a pin drop. The Jurors had already seen and heard the evidence, but now it was time to put all the pieces together. The Defense Attorney had little evidence to argue, but he tried, using new strategies to get the attention of the Jury. Would it work?

When the verdict was read, there was no outburst, just tears of relief streaming down the faces of family, friends, law enforcement officials and media who were all joyful that the man who so violently murdered Marlys would never again take the life of anyone. Two days later at sentencing, this was sealed with a life term in prison, consecutive to the one he is now serving for murdering Diane Edwards, his last victim.

Yes there is baggage, lots of it with the death of a child. Some emotions take a lot longer to sort through and put into the proper place. It took me nineteen years, five months and eight days (to sentencing) to sort through my quest for justice. The sorting was not easy but it had to be done. Coming face to face with the murderer was necessary in our case and so was the moral victory for Marlys. Baggage yes; it must be dealt with no matter how long it takes; it must be faced. Healing only takes place fully when we sort and clear whatever is keeping us from being the whole person that we want to be —for me, in memory of my beloved daughter.

5

Patio Talk

On a warm Sunday evening, Jack and I sat on our patio under the awning protecting us from the gentle rain coming down. We were reflecting as we often do about our children. Jack wondered where Marlys fit in now, because for so many years we had been consumed with solving her murder. We no longer had to deal with law enforcement or unanswered questions. Now that the trial was behind us, where was Marlys in this big family picture?

Of course, Marlys is still the second oldest even though we will always remember her as being only 18. During this conversation, the pain welled up inside of me again, like it does from time to time, even after so many years. Why have we been denied having such a beautiful person here with us? Why doesn't the pain go away? Those questions do have simple answers. An evil person took her life and because we love her, that pain will always be deep down inside no matter

52

how many years pass. I was reminded of an article I read which told of a mother who went to her child's grave for 50 years. So that answers the question of our pain: it never goes away.

Jack and I continued to reflect on Marlys and our other children. We knew we could call or visit any of them and, thankfully, they could call or visit us. We do not have that luxury with Marlys. She is in another life, one we don't understand. I told Jack how I continue to look for signs, make up stories, create ideas of ways that Marlys may be trying to let us know that she is with us still —we just can't see her. We talked about the butterflies, the gentle breeze like the touch of an angel, the fragrance of a rose, a whisper or something that reminds us of Marlys. Then our thoughts went to our upcoming trip.

Jack had seen an ad in a magazine and asked me with excitement saying, "How would you like to do something crazy?" Of course I wouldn't say yes until I knew what it was. His "crazy" idea turned out to be a *once in a lifetime* trip for us, fulfilling a dream that we have both had for at least 30 years. We would make a pilgrimage to Switzerland, to go to the Hospice at the Grande Saint Bernard Pass. Years ago, Jack and I met, each holding a Saint Bernard on the end of a leash. Both of us had dreamed of going to where the Saints began. With excitement we made reservations and set aside one special day on the tour to go to the Hospice, to spend the night. Excitedly we talked of seeing the dogs, meeting the Monks and visiting the museum where they have Barry, the Saint who is credited with saving many peoples lives who were crossing the Alps back in the 1800s.

Earlier, I had showed Jack the words on a tray that I have had for years, with pictures of Saint Bernards on it and a saying that the Saints go back to the early Christian era. Jack commented that he wasn't really sure they were 2000 years old. There we sat on the patio, with the rain coming even harder now. I said, with tears streaming down my face, "maybe I can go and sit on a hill and hug a Saint Bernard like I used to when I felt sad back in the '70s. But, since it may be cold, perhaps I'll just hug Barry in the museum."

Jack asked, "Where are our Saint Books?" Because we used to raise and show Saint Bernards, we had quite a collection. I told him they were on the book shelf in the basement family room. So off he went to find the books to answer some of our questions about just when the Saints came to the Hospice at the Grande Saint Bernard Pass. When he returned to the patio, he was holding a sheet of notebook paper with writing on it. It was a report Marlys had written for a class in grade school on Barry, the famous Saint Bernard. My tears continued, but they were happy tears now. A message from Marlys again. The paper was not in a book but between two St. Bernard books. Even after many moves —seven different houses in three different states— that report was still with us, waiting for the right time to appear.

Yes, I will hug a Saint Bernard in Switzerland. I might even cry, but I will remember Marlys and I will be happy.

* * * * * * *

I wrote the above reflection before we went to Switzerland. Little did I know the bitter sweet joy of being with the Saint Bernards at the Hospice at the Grande Saint Bernard Pass. Tears flowed with joy because I never thought I would have this opportunity to go there, even though I had dreamed of doing so. Then the tears flowed with sadness. I saw so many Saints who resembled Patience, my Saint who was locked in my bedroom during Marlys' attack. This breed has a natural instinct to rescue, and yet, because Patience was locked in my bedroom, she was unable to be with Marlys and possibly fight off her attacker. Patience knew the danger, heard the horror and died of a broken heart six months after the assault. For me the baggage tucked deep down inside has now been resolved when I cried with the Saints in a place of refuge far away and yet so close at heart.

When Sadness Overtakes Me

Why does sadness overtake me without warning after so many years? Sometimes it hits hard and I wonder what triggered that awful feeling. Who said what or what happened? Others may ask you the same question.

Sadness is an emotion we cannot control. Emotions are intense feelings that pop up when we least expect it and certainly we cannot keep them from happening.

When sadness hits me, I am often caught off guard —with a group of friends or just alone going about my own business. I try to understand that I have every right to be sad —my child is dead. But I don't want these feelings to dominate my life and make me miserable. I want to recognize this as a natural response to the emptiness I now feel without Marlys. Recognizing this gives me the strength and courage to work on the sad feelings and try to replace them with happier memories. Now that I know I have a right to be sad, I know I have that same right to be happy again.

Marlys would want that for me.

What Am I Supposed To look Like?

"I'm glad to meet you, Fran. Gee, I would never have guessed that you lost a child. You look great."

Many times I have heard words similar to these. Am I supposed to look different? Am I supposed to go along life's journey forever looking like I am in pain?

Well, I don't believe that I should look any different than Mrs. Fortunate, who still has her child or children, all healthy and alive. Yes, the pain was written all over my face for weeks, months, maybe even years, but through this pain and as healing began, there emerged peace and even happiness. I know there are days that I feel at least 150 years old. I've seen the pain of the death of my beloved child written in huge letters all over me. But I surely don't want to be this way. The grief stricken, still want to live —to be alive— to remember the fun times of days gone by. I tried, and this is a real effort, to be happy again. This need is alive within us, deep down, being bruised by pain, and it only came out when I began to see the love and concern of those around me. This will to be happy once again —because Marlys wants me to be— becomes strong and even powerful. At times maybe I do look great. For at least a moment, the pain is gone and I am myself once again.

Generally, the public does not see me cry. But there are times when my feelings overtake me, wherever I am, in church, at the grocery store. I am human, I haven't grown cold, I haven't forgotten the death of my daughter, but I am going on with life. The pain and emptiness without Marlys at times is unbearable, but I really believe that her desire for me to be happy is equally as strong, and for that reason I can say that I will be happy again.

Crushed or Polished

I heard this little statement somewhere, and I want to share it here. I don't know who wrote it, but it spoke to me. I hope the author doesn't mind it being used in this reflection.

It goes as follows:

These are the windstorms of our lives,
the tumblers of our lives
Life has put us through a tumbler.
We either come out crushed or polished.

Yes I can come out either crushed or polished by my grief. I could be totally crushed and give up. I am sure every bereaved parent would agree that giving up could be easy. We've all thought of surrendering to our pain. But, would my child want me to be crushed?

Knowing Marlys and the way she loved life, I am certain that she would want me to survive this tragedy and, yes —someday be polished. In the early months and even years of my bereavement, being polished sounded impossible, but as I struggled along with other bereaved friends, I found that yes I did start to shine again. Shine, yes shine, I sparkled like a polished gemstone! I smiled, I helped others, I started to heal. When I looked back over the torturous paths of the preceding months, I found that bit-by-bit I had been polished ever so gently by those I have touched and those who have touched me as well. Being polished does not mean that I no longer miss and long for my child. Not being crushed means that I have found a way to make my life worth while again and by doing so I give honor to my daughter.

Time Flies

I have said at one time or another that "time flies". Well sometimes I realize it flies by faster than I could even imagine. It seems that after Marlys died, I found myself wondering where the years have gone. How long has it been since I was able to hug or talk to her? It is almost as though I have a new calendar now —divided between when Marlys was here on earth and everything that has happened since she died.

Just recently, I was reflecting on life in general, preparing for a meeting. My thoughts went back to when Marlys was with me. I realized that the life that I have been living had been suddenly changed. Yes I see life as "before Marlys' death" and "after Marlys' death." The clock has stood still for Marlys —I still see her as she was in 1979, just a young woman of eighteen years of age. When I think about my family now, I realize that Marlys would now be much older, still between Ray and Lynn. To look at time in another way, my younger daughter Lynn has reached the age Jack was in 1979. Her middle daughter, Crystal, is, as I write this, the same age that Marlys will always be. How can this be?

Time does fly and life does go on. Not the way I would have wanted it to, but as I learned when I lived near the ocean, time and tide waits for no one. The family grows up on its new calendar. Even the grandchildren, who obviously never got to meet Marlys, have learned that we have a different calendar because I will always remember Marlys.

Healing started to take place when I began to realize that life is different now and always will be. When I look at what is different, I realize how I have been affected by this enormous loss, a tragedy that should never have happened. When I start to seek memories and intertwine them with my "new calendar", I realize that the child I loved is not lost —only out of sight. When I keep her memory alive, Marlys is but a thought away. What I once loved, I will never loose. My daughter continues to be a very important part of my life. It is just a different calendar.

Yes, time does fly, but never too fast for me to remember Marlys.

6

Look Up

Do I look down from a mountain or do I look up? My response is, it depends on whether I am at the top or at the bottom of the mountain. When I am in grief, where am I? At the bottom of the mountain or at the top?

Being at the top of a mountain looking all around at the beauty of nature can be an awesome experience, but it can also be scary. I have been in Switzerland on a mountain so high small aircraft flew below me in the valleys. I feel dizzy when I look down from the top of a mountain. I am afraid of heights and feel like I am going to fall. It's a long way to the bottom.

It is the same when I am at the bottom of a mountain, looking up. The mountain is still so beautiful and majestic, but there is a long, steep road ahead to get to the top. I will need a lot of energy and time to get up there. In some cases it takes more than a little skill.

This image of a mountain tells me exactly where I am when I am in mourning —a long way from the other end, whether it be looking up or looking down. Grief, however, does not give us an opportunity to enjoy the view of that majestic mountain because that panorama is blurred by tears. It is hard to look up when my pain is so intense I can hardly lift my head. Likewise, if I am looking down, my sorrow is still nearly unbearable. Not only do I see the weeds and rocks that are under my feet, I feel like I will fall if I try to do anything out of the ordinary. I hesitate to do something as simple as taking a step. How can I ever see the majestic views from the mountain again? How can I look up and see the beauty that surrounds me?

Friends who are fellow travelers give me that chance to look up. I meet someone who has made progress on that rocky road of healing. They hold out a hand for me. I look down and see that someone has placed a cup of tea beside me, handed me a book to read or sent me a note saying "thinking of you." Am I looking up or looking down? Wherever I am and however I feel right now, there is a friend waiting to help me up that mountain, waiting to guide me back down that rocky path over that uneven ground called grief. She or he is waiting so that when I am ready I will see that I am not alone.

Sharing

Sharing is a sacred thing, coming from the depths of the heart. When I share my thoughts and feelings with others, I open up a part of me that is fragile, a part of me that has been wounded beyond belief. Sharing pain is not easy for most people. It hurts too much.

Why would we want to bring up things that make us feel sad? Since I began to attend bereavement support groups in 1983, I have been sharing with people, all over the country actually, listening to their stories and telling mine. I have found that in that sharing —sometimes with people I don't even know, my pain and theirs has been lifted, ever so slightly, and perhaps only for just a few minutes. It is worth it, even for only a moment of relief.

I often tell people that when we listen to another person tell her or his story, we are not thinking about ourselves at that moment, and that is the beginning of our own healing process —part of our grief work. Knowing that others hurt as I do, for some reason makes sense, and puts me on the right track. They understand what I am talking about and I understand what they are saying. We join to make sense out of the unthinkable.

For a long time I worked with a Compassionate Friends chapter in Delaware County, Pennsylvania, just outside Philadelphia. It proved to be a wonderful place for me to continue my grief work during the time I was also dealing with an unsolved murder. My friends there shared my pain with me, despite that anguish being ever so consuming. Even though at times I was the chapter leader, this loving and caring group of bereaved parents and siblings understood I was "still" a bereaved parent. They reached out to me where I was at that time. They never passed judgment and said "I should be over it by now" nor did they back away because I was in a leadership role.

Those friends who I was surrounded by for seven good years became a wonderful accepting family. I am grateful for the time I have spent with all of them, during the good times and the not so good. It was in that sharing that we all grew together. My heart will be with them and I will always remember their love and compassion. I stay in contact with many of these friends, and they have affirmed me returning home to Minnesota and my place in the country.

Love Grows On A Hill

When I was still in Pennsylvania, I received a little brochure from my former church in Afton, Minnesota, where Marlys was buried in 1979. The brochure was asking for donations for memorial gifts for a new sanctuary. On the front of the brochure it said "Love Grows On The Hill." That message stuck with me when I revisited the church on Dedication Sunday while on a visit to

Minnesota to see my two surviving children and my grandchildren.

The phrase "Love Grows On The Hill" came to me many times during the week. Mother's Day approached. Mother's Day is a dreaded time for me because it will always be a reminder of Marlys' death. She was pronounced dead on May 10th and buried on May 12th, which was the day before Mother's Day in 1979. That year when I visited the church, Mother's Day fell on May 14th, but the actual date is not important. The second Sunday in May is always filled with sadness and longing. During that week leading up to Mother's Day, the phrase "Love Grows On The Hill" became "Love Grows In Sharing With Friends."

The overwhelming love that grows within a bereavement support group is hard to comprehend. It is a love that only bereaved friends can understand. All of us have so many hills to climb and sometimes we tumble down, but there is a friend either at the top or at or near the bottom to take my hand. It doesn't matter where I am on that up and down cycle, there is always someone nearby at just the right time. Love does grow everywhere, on the hill, and at the bottom, the top and half way up.

Love grows with those who are striving to help others.

Photographs

Photographs of Marlys are so very precious! Never again will I be able to tell her to stand over by Ray and Lynn so I can take their picture. The slides and photos taken years ago help our family feel her presence and yet we long for Marlys to be with us. Individual shots of Marlys doing special things are also ever so close to my heart. All photos of her have become one of a kind —the moment never to be captured again.

Lynn, two years younger than Marlys made a video a few years ago including photos she could find of Marlys, Ray and herself as young children to surprise me. The video had a beautiful song playing as the pictures one by one flashed on the screen. Lynn gave this to me for Mother's Day. The video ended with me sitting in a field of Daffodils.

Bringing together good memories when we look at pictures from the past, helps to fill the void, if just for a moment. Pictures of a beautiful young woman will always bring joy —of her growing up until the last one at age 18. Marlys will forever be young; we remember her smile.

The Secret Gift

I used to have a secret pal. I don't hear much about secret pals anymore, but when I was young it was very popular. Each person would draw a name from a 'hat' and the person whose name we drew would be our secret pal for a period of time, like six months or a year. During that time, we would send a note of friendship, signing it "your secret pal." Each person would receive small acts of kindness through these notes during that period. At the end, I usually gave a small gift to acknowledge that I was their secret pal. I always had fun trying to guess who was doing these nice things for me during the months or year.

My bereaved friends are like secret pals. In the beginning I did not know who these people were, but small acts of kindness —notes, cards, phone calls started to come and soon— when I started to heal, I found out who my secret pals were who had been helping me along the way. Now I can put a face to the name and I was welcomed with the gift of friendship. No longer was I alone, guessing who these people were in my life. I now know that these friends are there for me even when I don't know who they are.

During a sharing session some time ago, one of the more newly bereaved mentioned that on the second anniversary of their child's death, only a few friends remembered to send cards. My response was simple. In time, perhaps this year, you will be getting cards and calls from friends you've made at the bereavement support group. You will have love and encouragement during these difficult times. We are there for you, during the meetings and as secret pals.

The Gift of Flowers

I know the pain and sorrow of having a child die and I have come to learn that little things mean so much to me now. So often in the past, I took these little things for granted. The small items were just part of life and sometimes I even passed them off as not important. Now, I am different. I know that the small events are the most important things that I could ever savor. Oh, if only I could hear the voice, see the smile, or feel the touch of my child.

When a friend or family member calls on the phone and says "I was just thinking about you," or when someone calls and compliments me on something I have done, or when I am handed a bouquet of flowers and butterflies, I feel special even though I may be having a bad day. Someone thought about me and it made me feel good. I feel that "yes" maybe life is worth living after all.

I realize that since Marlys died, I have good days and bad days, even after many years. It does not seem to matter how many years have passed, I still love and miss my daughter. The fact that I cannot reach out and hug her tugs at my heart sometimes until I think it will surely break.

When I am feeling down, feeling sad, missing my child, I remember the little things that meant so much when she was here with me. The little treasures that I have in my memory, are what is important.

The little dandelion flower lovingly picked with the broken stem, oh how very special are those little flowers —treasures from the heart. They are reminders that "yes" life is special because I did have those riches and they can never be taken away.

So as I remember those little things, I am thankful and share them with others. It's the sweet memories that matter. It is true, I can make a difference in someone else's life.

7

Grief Is The Price We Pay

We hear the words often in our support group meetings that grief is the price we pay for loving our children and siblings. If I had not loved so deeply, there would be no pain. Grief is not a sign of weakness but a human emotion that must be dealt with in order for me to once again laugh and enjoy life. Sometimes that seems almost impossible, but over time and with hard work, I actually do feel the warm breeze and find joy. I see the butterfly and reach to touch it, look for signs of an angel's touch, see the rose and bend to smell it. When I hear a funny story, I actually laugh. I even reach out my hand to help another grieving person over those rough stepping stones of grief.

Grief is not to be feared, but to be challenged. Am I to let it rule me like an ugly tyrant or am I willing to try to understand and sort out that grief? It is so important to recognize that I mourn because I have loved and still love my child who is no longer with me on this earth. I need to know that I can become whole again as I face each day with hope because my helping friends are with me. As days turn into months and years, I have turned my grief into a life filled with love, if for no other reason than that I loved Marlys so-o-o much! There can be no greater honor for my child than to live a good life in service to others who need my healing touch.

There Can Be No Rainbow

There is an American Indian proverb that says "There can be no rainbow for the soul if the eyes did not have tears." When I look at the rainbow in the sky, I see the beauty of the colors unfolding when the rainbow appears. The rainbow follows the rain, sometimes very heavy rain, when the sun bursts forth in the sky. It is then the beauty of that rainbow somehow makes me smile and even feel good at that moment after the downpour.

So it was when my life was shattered by the death of my daughter. The tears flowed, the storms were rough, the roads were muddy, everything seemed to be drenched with sorrow and pain. But when I started to look for meaning in life again and reach out to others, I saw a glimmer of that rainbow —far in the distance. I wanted to experience more of the rainbow, the beautiful colors, the awesome beauty that my eyes could not believe I was seeing. But it was difficult; I couldn't find the sun, let alone the rainbow. Tears were still in my eyes. My soul searched for new meaning, a reason to live again, something that would give me hope that I would smile again, that I will be happy somehow. Is it possible? In support groups I found that others too were searching for that glimmer of hope that would keep them going. The tears in their eyes are just like my tears —lamentations of pain so deep that others just don't understand why we are not back to normal, living the way we used to before tragedy struck. But I know I will never be the same as I was when Marlys was here on earth with me. When I reach out to other bereaved parents, the rainbow starts to appear again. But this time it has new meaning. Because of the accompaniment with each other, at meetings, by phone, over a cup of coffee or tea, I try to be the sun for others. I understand that I would not have seen the true beauty of that rainbow if my eyes had not had those tears. We all share the pain as well as the joy. And so it is true, "There can be no rainbow for the soul if the eyes did not have tears."

Sunday Morning TV

Sunday morning TV is usually filled with preachers from various denominations shouting away to get their message out to their intended audience. At home when I lived in Pennsylvania, I could usually find the morning news while I prepared breakfast before going to church.

One morning however, I was visiting in Minnesota before I moved back to my place in the country, without cable TV. All I could receive were the local channels. They all seemed to have preachers giving their messages. I flipped through the channels looking for the news. I saw a familiar face —Art Linkletter— a "star" from my past. Art was a man I looked up to as a young adult because he seemed kind. When he told his story that day, I was fascinated by the message that he brought. Like in the past, he was filled with humor in everything he was saying and yes, he was on one of those preaching shows.

Art started out by saying that he was very smart from the very beginning, stating that he was born in Canada and "chose" to be adopted by a couple from California, where it is much warmer. The family that adopted him was in the ministry and were poor. He said he remembers living in the back of houses —addresses being in half numbers. They even had a smaller house behind theirs, which I laughingly understood to mean the outhouse. He quickly added that the Rockafellers had come through Canada a few days earlier, but he chose another loving family to be his.

I continued preparing breakfast and became more and more interested in what Art was saying. Where was he leading the audience? Then, Art Linkletter began to talk about his daughter who committed suicide after taking LSD when she was nineteen-years-old. He told about how angry he was at the person who supplied her with the stuff and how enraged he was at everything concerning her death. He told how this fury was consuming him. Then one day, he decided to try to make a difference in this cold, cruel world. He became involved with World Vision, did mission work, became active in getting the message out about drugs. Helping Others! Wow, did that message hit a golden key in my heart that Sunday morning. Helping others! Isn't that what I am supposed to do and have been doing? Isn't that what I am called to do? When my eyes are open, so to speak, I have a mission in life. It is not to sit back and be a "couch potato." My personal mission is to reach out to those who need me. In that reaching out, I am made whole again.

Art Linkletter said that he was "86 years old and going strong." He was not sitting back doing nothing. This good man was still reaching out to comfort and console grieving parents after so many years. He is an example of what I can also do for the bereaved. Young and old alike, I can make a difference in the lives of those who need me most —the grieving and hurting in my midst. So I will follow my heart and follow Art Linkletter.

Is There Magic?

Is there magic in what I do in honor and memory of my daughter when I work to make the bereavement support group a success? I don't always know when what I do touches someone else in a special way on their healing path. Art Linkletter doesn't know how he lifted my spirits that Sunday morning, because I didn't write to him. Sometimes, however, I do share my appreciation, especially when the contact has been face to face.

Before Marlys was murdered, I had a tradition of giving each of my children an ornament for the Christmas tree each year. When she died, I didn't know what to do with her ornaments, so I hung them on the tree, feeling sad that no more were being added. In time I began to attend memorial services for bereavement groups. I would receive an ornament with my child's name on it as a token of remembrance. One year I decided to decorate a small artificial tree, with tiny white lights, and I put all of Marlys' ornaments on the tree. It made me feel good to see them on her special tree. I kept the tree up all year because it gave me comfort knowing that these memorial ornaments were not packed away in a box, forgotten until next year. And I shared that practice with others.

Here is a note giving one person's response to what I did.

Dear Fran,

I'm writing to thank you and all of the active members of The Compassionate Friends for remembering my son's anniversary in your newsletter. Also, let me tell you how your kindness helped me to commemorate our Bernie's passing.

On October 26th, I set up a little table in front of the fireplace. My daughter made a wreath of moss and leaves, and we laid it on the table with Bernie's picture in the center, the little crocheted angel with his name, and the candle from last year's memorial service.

It was such a great comfort to me and I want to thank you all.

Warmest regards, Nancy.

Can you see the magic? Healing comes from doing nice things for others in memory of our loved ones. Holidays, birthdays, anniversaries are all special times when I can extend compassion and make some magic. I tried extra hard to make that holiday season one of many magic moments as I offered my compassion in the memory of my child.

A Stranger in Paradise

Not long ago, I found it easy to talk to a stranger who remembered the story of a teenager murdered not far from Walter Mondale's home. Sean had seen the TV Show *48 Hours* that told Marlys' unsolved murder story. He continued to ask questions apologizing each time for bringing it up. "I hope you don't mind," he would say and I encouraged him to ask.

A small world, from Afton, Minnesota to Los Cabos, Mexico, but Sean remembered the story. Is there closure? How long did it take the cops to find the killer?

When I answered each question, he became more agitated —really not wanting the truth of what actually happened. When I told him I found Marlys in my home, tears filled his eyes and he backed away. "I can't hear anymore," he said. "I have a four year old daughter and I could not imagine what you have gone through".

We never want anyone to have to go through what we faced, but this man was typical of those on the outside, as we call them. A person on TV is a long way from the reality of sitting at a table with the person's mother. We can separate ourselves from the pain we see on TV. To come face to face with reality —looking into a mother's eyes, Sean faced a reality he could not imagine. He couldn't comprehend how anyone could survive as a parent. He understood there is no closure.

At the end of our meeting, he was still focused on Marlys' murder, while I had brought up another subject, having him show us more of the resort, that he had forgotten already. Finally, we walked along the paths, past flowers and shrubs. Butterflies of all colors surrounded us. I knew and felt Marlys' presence, and hoped Sean would be more aware of the evil in this world because of our encounter. Maybe he was lead by butterflies to help him go beyond a program on television to the actual human experience.

Yearning

Especially in the early months after Marlys died, I found myself looking for her. I tried to believe this nightmare was only in a dream and I would wake up to find her alive. I found myself following little white Datsun B-210s like she owned in 1979. I once followed a car like hers to the Afton Post Office, only to see another young girl hop out of the car and go into the Post Office. Crazy, you say. Yes, maybe, but I desperately wanted to wake up and find Marlys still alive.

Seeing young blonde girls in the supermarket brought tears to my eyes, again. I wished they would turn around and one would be Marlys.

These thoughts and wishes are not rational, but what is sane when tragedy strikes in such a horrendous way? They are part of the denial I had to work through. It takes more than simply stating that my child is dead to make it real. Denial is my cry that it can't be true.

In time I learned that having these thoughts is normal. The bereaved parent is in shock in the early weeks and months. This shock protected me from going insane, so when I searched for the unreal, I was not crazy —just craving that hug and searching with all my heart to find it.

8

Fly Like a Bird

One morning while I prepared for the day and fixed breakfast for Jack and myself, I heard a song that really caught my attention. Boz Scaggs was a guest on the *Good Morning America* show and was promoting one of his recent recordings. The song was quite lively with a Cajun flair —especially good to get me moving in the morning. Not only was the rhythm catchy, but the words stuck in my head and would not leave me all that day and for several days to follow.

The music reminded me immediately of my Granny who was so much a part of my life as I grew up. Maybe it was the happy sounds that I remember from Granny when she would come across the field from her home to mine, whistling to the top of her voice. Granny always sounded happy even when I knew she wasn't. Granny's life was not easy, but she made the best of every day, proclaiming life was good through the sounds she shared with the world.

When I heard the words Boz Scaggs sang, I could just picture Granny saying those same words, "Some times I cry, sometimes I fly like a bird". What a contrast, what a comparison, but so real in life. You see, my Granny's oldest son Norwood died at age twenty-one in a single car crash in 1928. My Granny knew the pain of losing a child. Tears would well up in her eyes whenever she talked about her son, taken at such a young age. Granny never forgot Norwood, no matter how many years had passed. Norwood was still very present in her life and in the lives of her other two children —my Uncle Wilton and my mother, Mildred.

Granny also knew the joy of "flying like a bird." Granny dedicated her life to helping others. Being a mid-wife, she found herself spending many nights away from her own family while she cared for women who needed her expertise. Granny sometimes would cry but yes she would "fly like a bird" when she brought joy and happiness, comfort and peace to others.

The words of a song, a voice from the past, tears and joy. All are mine to look at or listen to —to find added meaning in my life. Yes, sometimes I cry, sometimes I fly like a bird! It's okay.

Sing and Dance

How can I ever sing and dance again? How can I ever even smile after my child has died? It took a long time for my pain to lessen, although it never will go away. Naturally I did not feel like dancing, singing or doing anything that brings pleasure. I actually felt uncomfortable thinking of merriment? Am I doing an injustice to my beloved Marlys who has died?

Now that Marlys' case was solved, Summer back in Minnesota is a real pleasure for me. I am no longer griped with fear from the unknown killer. I can actually enjoy the woods, the country life and the peacefulness that reminds me of the days long ago when Marlys was still here with me.

Melanie, my oldest granddaughter, graduated from high school in the year 2000. Of course there was a great celebration for her special day. I told a few of my friends that I would be dancing and that I would dance two special songs for Marlys. She loved to dance and Marlys would be dancing along with the rest of the family at the first chance she got. I admit I did dance to a number of songs but two were especially in memory of Marlys. That would be her way of giving a gift to Melanie —having me dance for her. I danced the first song, *A Good Hearted Woman*, in a group of guys and gals all around me.

Karoke had not been invented when Marlys was alive but since it came along, I had wanted to try it. So did my daughter, Lynn, but Lynn was a little bit shy. My son Ray was an old pro at Karoke. Ray has a great voice and an unbelievable memory for the words. He doesn't need the lyrics which appear on the screen in front of you when you are singing. Ray has so much confidence he made Lynn and I want to try our turn at singing along with the music. And sure enough Lynn and I got the courage to do so. We sang *Pretty Woman* which was the second of Marlys' favorite songs. There in the circle of family and friends I found singing and dancing like it should have been all these years.

The sweet memories and the happy celebration of a young girl, Marlys' niece, graduating from high school made it fun to dance and sing. Melanie was the star that night, but Marlys was shining her light on all of us saying "Mom, be happy," saying Ray, Lynn, Jack be happy! Sing and dance! I am with you and always will be.

Sad Songs

I'm sure many people are familiar with the singer/song writer Elton John. He has written quite a few songs that are very popular today. One of the songs he wrote several years ago has words that struck a note in my heart when I heard them. The song is entitled *Sad Songs*. I stopped and listened to words of the song and thought that maybe he had experienced pain similar to mine. What inspired him to write the song? Some people listen to the music and ignore the words. I listen to the words but Jack just hears the music generally.

In *Sad Songs*, I could not help but listen carefully to what was being said. I was reminded of so many bereavement support group sessions.

In the lyrics, Elton John writes that "sad songs say so much. If someone else is suffering enough to write it down, every single word makes sense and it's easier to have that song around."

The stories that I hear in sharing sessions also say so much. Every single word people speak makes sense because my suffering has brought me to understand that others know what is on my heart. I get together with others because they understand. Sad songs say so much and sad stories say so much. Both speak of love that will never be forgotten —love that will always be with me— deep down in my heart. Because I have suffered so much, I can write it down, I can tell my story and every single word makes sense.

I am not afraid to let those thoughts and words be part of my life. I never know when I have touched another person with deep love and compassion.

Healing Tears

I have heard people say that tears are healing. At times that makes sense to me and at other times I wonder.

A few years ago, I had the joy and pleasure of attending my younger daughter Lynn's pinning ceremony when she became a Registered Nurse. I felt all the joy and happiness a parent can have from the success and hard work that she put in to achieve this wonderful goal. I took pride in knowing that Lynn was achieving one of the goals

I had when I was young. I truly am proud of her, and some of the tears I had were tears of joy for her.

But I had other tears. I cried because Lynn's sister, Marlys, could not be there to share the joy of Lynn receiving her pin. I have a good life now, but that does not mean that I have gotten over my loss. It does not mean that I forget. Life goes on and the events that are important now —so many years after that terrible death— are also events that I wish I could have shared with my dead child.

Marlys was murdered three weeks before her class graduated from High School. When I attended Lynn's high school graduation in 1981, I expected to be sad but I wasn't. Perhaps I was still in the early stages of grief, but Lynn is not Marlys and I have tried very hard to keep that in mind. I love both my daughters, and my son. I know they are each separate individuals. So that's why, maybe, that Lynn's High School graduation was happy, not terribly sad.

So why the tears in 1996? I think the answer is that I was sad that Marlys couldn't be with me to share the joy of Lynn's achievement. Lynn told me that part of the reason she worked so hard and succeeded in nursing school was that she wanted to honor and acknowledge Marlys. Lynn remembered a long time ago, barely in her teens, when her favorite stuffed animal was torn. When Lynn came home from school the next day, it was fixed, with a note from "Doctor" Marlys, telling Lynn to be happy. Lynn, her brother Ray and I rejoice in Lynn's successes. The three of us shed a tear for the one who is missing, who isn't here to share it with us.

Going forward in life as a healed bereaved parent means that I will experience events that are important, and often I will remember that my loved one has been deprived of that experience. This is when a tear will come. It is also a time to acknowledge my joy in knowing the memory will always be with me. And that is healing too.

Song Sung Blue

Neil Diamond sings a song with the words "Song sung blue, Everybody knows one." There are many songs written out of pain —pain from the sadness in our heart of having a loved one die.

Songs often speak to me and when I listen carefully —getting in touch with my own feelings as I listen to the words. Singing along to happy sounds but often relating the music to my feelings of emptiness bringing tears.

Listening carefully to music can be a very healing experience. Whether the words are happy or sad, that music can put me on the road to healing. Tears are healing and so are the cheerful sounds that bring back memories of Marlys.

Remembering a favorite joyful song or hearing a song sung blue, I can sing and capture a feeling that my daughter is always near when I listen with my heart.

9

Alive In Our Hearts

My child is alive in my heart each time I see a butterfly, feel a gentle breeze from an angel or smell a fragrant rose. These are the good moments —the happy memories. As the months and years go by, it seems that I search even more to find these moments —to remember Marlys as she was when she was here with me.

When I see the flowers springing from the ground and the sunny skies of Spring, I remember the sunshine that once filled my heart through my daughter and remember that sunshine now because memories never leave me and neither does the love that I shared with her. Remember —what we love, we never lose.

Nice People

Some of the nicest people I have ever known I met at bereavement support groups. When my friends and family forsake me because I am different now, a new circle of people are there for me. For example, The Compassionate Friends is an international, non-denominational, non-sectarian self-help group whose members truly show love and compassion for all who gather at the meetings. To me, this love and compassion is like the hands of an angel reaching out through each bereaved person, touching another —showing love and offering hope. Those bereaved who are further down the road of healing offer hope and understanding to those with a grief so fresh there seems to be no hope.

Because of this compassion I have learned from other bereaved friends, my daughter's life is honored in a way that gives her death meaning. My heart is opened to a new understanding —that pain exists because I will forever miss Marlys. But, her love will also never leave me. The road may be rocky with hills and valleys, sometimes steep and long, but together we can make it. I know how to feel the love, and, in doing so, my daughter is ever present with me. I will continue to look for that butterfly, angel, and rose; I feel the love that will never be taken from me.

Red Hearts On The Tree

Red Hearts lovingly trimmed with gold, were hand painted by half a dozen bereaved parents in The Delaware County Compassionate Friends Chapter we helped organize. The tree full of red hearts (226 total) recounted the pain of each family who had been touched by that group in four short years.

We held an Annual Memorial Service on the first Sunday in December, to honor the memory of our children, siblings and grandchildren before the rush of the holiday consumed everyone. I believe it is crucial to dedicate this time each year on the first Sunday of December, and take comfort in knowing that this is a special event for all bereaved who have come together over the past year. When we do this we make a "Tradition." We did it once, on our first December, and we all liked what we did and so the tradition continues.

Red Hearts tell the story of the love we have for those who could not be with us for that holiday season. *Red Hearts*, a reminder that our children, siblings, grandchildren, nieces and nephews will always be in our hearts, and no one can ever take that away from us. Families are together, maybe only on that day, listening to a message, hearing a poem, listening to the words of a song, wiping a tear, lighting a candle —all part of remembering. And, after it is over, a hug from a parent, a child, a grandparent was passed on and on. Love radiated throughout the room as everyone felt the presence of love in the memories that were still alive in our hearts. That love in our hearts, represented by the little *Red Hearts* on the tree, will last forever.

Friends

Marlys had lots of friends —too many for me to name. Her wallet was filled with their photos, most with notes to her on the back of the picture. She carried them with her in her purse wherever she went. These photos were in her purse at her feet on that fatal day when she was so brutally attacked in our home.

Some of these pals had shared time with Marlys outside on the warm grass at lunch on May 8, 1979. The girls were laughing and telling stories —memories only they can treasure now. Marlys gave them a ride to their home after school as she always did —none of them knowing it would be the last time they would see her alive.

These classmates were determined to find the murderer, kept in contact with law enforcement, bugging them to never give up. Marlys' girl friends put up posters, gathered reward money and kept seeking justice just like they were family.

Young teens, devastated by this untimely death kept Marlys' memory alive in the St. Croix Valley. Buddies at school, at the little cafe, during the long investigation, now grown and have children of their own. Friends then, and now, through all eternity.

Moving Marlys

Memorial Lutheran Church (the Little White Church on the hill as it was known by all who lived in the St. Croix Valley) was the church I attended when my children were growing up. This is where Marlys and her sister Lynn and brother Ray were confirmed. Next to the little white church were two cemeteries —one called The Evergreen Cemetery (a community cemetery) and the other belonged to the church. When Marlys died in May 1979 I called to see if there was space available in the church cemetery. There were a few lots left so I buried her there after the funeral the day before Mothers Day. It was a place I could go, place flowers and cry. The setting was beautiful, towering above the beautiful blue St. Croix River which Marlys dearly loved.

One and a half years later with the murder still unsolved, Jack and I moved my two surviving children and his three children to the East Coast. The daily reminders of the murder and the fear that gripped me was too much to bear. The decision to move away was not too hard but still painful.

The children adjusted as best they could in our new home in Pennsylvania, but I was 1200 miles from Marlys' grave. I could not place flowers on special days so I cried about that as well.

Over four years passed and Jack and I discussed the possibility of moving Marlys' grave East near where we lived. I found a very nice church cemetery on a hill overlooking the Great Valley near Valley Forge in Malvern, Pennsylvania. This spot was lovely so we decided to proceed with the move. I contacted Memorial Lutheran Church in

Afton, Minnesota and also the mortuary that handled her burial there. A mortuary in Malvern was taking care of the move on the Pennsylvania end. I decided to leave her stone in Afton so her friends would have a place to go to remember.

Our pastor, family members and a few friends were with us when her earthly body was placed in this new grave. As time went by, Jack and I decided we would be buried next to Marlys so we put our stone there too.

Then, after getting justice for Marlys in 1998 and more justice in 2000, Jack and I started talking again about a move. This time back to Minnesota, the place I call home. We began our search for a house, looking in an area about an hour North of Afton. I really didn't feel right moving back to that area which would still have constant reminders of Marlys' death. As luck would have it, we found a large piece of property (18.83 acres) with a house, a creek running through the property and 787 feet of lake front. Wow! We decided to divide the property so we could build a one level home for our future. That in itself was a challenge but we were able to get all the proper permits, build a road across the creek and build our dream home overlooking the lake.

Finding my place in the country was a very happy time but Marlys' grave remained in Pennsylvania. The search for a place to bring Marlys' grave led me to the Long Lake Community Cemetery where I purchased three plots. The cemetery is almost directly across the lake from our new home. On the last day of

Victims' Awareness Week, April 27, 2002, Marlys' earthly body was reintered back home in Minnesota. Marlys' special friends, our family and our friends were all present.

At the gathering back at our new home, friends remembered Marlys, paging through her year book filled with messages of love and compassion, precious memories.

The stones for her grave and ours arrived in May just in time for putting flowers out. Now her family can visit her grave again, place butterflies, angels and roses as decorations, and always remember her with love.

Butterflies, Angels and Roses

Now that my work on this book is nearly done, I am at peace. I hope that my readers will share in the peace and healing I've experienced. The future is most important now, because I am content with the past.

Butterflies can be a part of your life too, as affirmations of when we do good things. They are our symbol of new life. When we put the dock in at our shoreline this Spring, the first Swallowtail butterfly of the season fluttered over the decking, as if to inspect and approve our work.

A few days ago, as I write this, a bereaved mother called, asked if she could stop in for a few minutes. I invited her into our house, sat with her as she talked about her daughter's death, two years ago, on Mother's day, May 11 that year. She knew of Marlys' story, shared the pain of her loss and mine, and thanked me for what I've done for grieving parents. "We can feel the spirit, just by sitting together," she said. "Our angels have visited us," I replied.

We planted roses by our gazebo, on Mother's Day, and somehow this year they are more fragrant and full than before.

Butterflies, angels and roses are forever a part of my life, with Jack, with Ray and Lynn and their families, and with a treasure chest of memories of Marlys.

Affirmation

Since moving Marlys' grave back to Minnesota, Jack and I formed a bereavement support group here in Isanti County. My daughter Lynn has joined us in our work and facilitates those whose brother or sister has died. Lynn is a registered nurse and is enthusiastic in taking part in this project, done in memory of Marlys.

We also try to keep up on the latest developments in grief work. At the time when I finished my work on this book, Lynn and Jack went to a conference offered by the Minnesota Coalition for Death Education and Support, to learn more about the latest in bereavement thinking. During one of the times they had the opportunity to talk together, Jack explained a bit about my writings to Lynn. He told her about the chapter devoted to songs that had meaning in my life.

Lynn asked if *Only The Good Die Young* was one of the songs. When he said it wasn't, she went on to tell him about how she and Marlys would ride up on the back of a convertible when she and Marlys were visiting their Dad in Texas. "We sang *Only The Good Die Young*." Jack had not heard that story.

When they got in the car to come home from the conference, Lynn turned on the radio. The first song they heard was *Only The Good Die Young*! Neither Lynn nor Jack had heard that song in years.

For a long time I have said I don't believe in coincidences, and that when things like this happen, it is a message or a sign that things are being done right. We had an affirmation from Marlys that she is with us and is pleased with the work we do in her memory. It is fitting that Marlys should have the last word.